Ray Manley's INDIAN LANDS

Text by Clara Lee Tanner

(A Gauche) CANYON DE CHELLY MONUMENT NATIONAL:
   LA MAISON BLANCHE (APPELÉE AUTREFOIS
   CASA BLANCA)
   (7 Photographies)

(左) キャニオン・デ シェイ 国有記念物内 白亜館

(Links) CANYON DE CHELLY NATIONAL MONUMENT: DAS
   WEIßE HAUS (FRÜHER CASA BLANCA GENANNT)
   (7 Bilder)

(Left) CANYON DE CHELLY NATIONAL MONUMENT,
   THE WHITE HOUSE (once called Casa Blanca)
Beginning about 1066, the Anasazi lived in this cave beneath cliffs
rising a thousand feet. The tapestry on the sandstone walls and fall
color give a final touch of beauty to this canyon wall.

(A Droite) LE CANARD SUR LE ROCHER

(右) 岩上 の あひる

(Rechts) DIE ENTE AUF DEM FELSEN

(Right) DUCK ON A ROCK
It often takes a little imagination to visualize many of the formations
by a name which is often less inspiring than the subject itself.

LE ROCHER DE L'ARAIGNÉE

蜘 蛛 岩

DER SPINNENSTEIN

SPIDER ROCK
This 800 foot spire is one of the most impressive
natural wonders of the major canyons. During the
spring and summer runoffs the canyon floors are
often covered with water. From walls over 1000 feet
above the canyon one can view this legendary
monument and appreciate its geological wonder.

(A Gauche) TROUPEAU DE MOUTONS NAVAJO
AU ROCHER GLISSANT

(A Droite) CHARRETTE NAVAJO

滑り岩附近 の ナヴァホ の羊群

(Links) NAVAJO SCHAFHERDE BEIM FELSENRUTSCH

(Left) NAVAJO FLOCK AT SLIDE ROCK
The Navajo began living in the canyon about 400 years after the
Anasazi abandoned the canyons. No more than 500 people have
occupied the canyons at one time.

ナヴァホ の 荷馬車

(Rechts) NAVAJOWAGEN

(Right) NAVAJO WAGON
This is an older photograph showing the Navajo returning to their
home in Canyon del Muerto, one of the three major canyons of the
area. After fall harvest, all the families leave the canyon, for its
temperature drops below zero in the winter. They return in the
spring to plant their various crops. Today the pickup truck has
replaced the wagon.

(*A Gauche*) LA MAISON DES ANTELOPES

カモシカの家

(*Links*) DAS ANTILOPENHAUS

(*Left*) ANTELOPE HOUSE
This ruin is one of the larger ones in Canyon del Muerto, named after the four antelope pictographs on the lower portion of its 600 foot high canyon walls.

(*A Droite*) RUINE DE LA MAISON DES MOMIES

(右) ミイラ館旧蹟

(*Rechts*) RUINE DES MUMIENHAUSES

(*Right*) MUMMY HOUSE RUINS
The earliest section of Mummy Cave are among the oldest ruins to be found in Canyon del Muerto. The four story tower was built about 1284 as indicated by tree ring dating.

(*Page 10*) TAOS PUEBLO, Nouveau Mexique

(十頁) タオス・プエブロ, ニュー・メキシコ州

(*Seite 10*) TAOS PUEBLO, New Mexico

(*Page 10*) TAOS PUEBLO, New Mexico
Ben Marcus, famous dancer, and his wife enjoy the morning sunshine. Though exposed to 400 years of Mexican, Spanish, and Anglo civilization, the Pueblo's culture has changed little. Ceremonial dances here are among the most precise and colorful of all the Pueblos.

(*Page 11*) CANYON DE CHACO, MONUMENT NATIONAL, Nouveau Mexique

(十一頁) チャコ・キャニオン国有記念物内 プエブロ・ボニト, ニュー・メキシコ州

(*Seite 11*) CHACO CANYON NATIONAL MONUMENT, New Mexico

(*Page 11*) CHACO CANYON NATIONAL MONUMENT, New Mexico
Prior to 1887 Pueblo Bonito was the world's largest apartment house according to Archaeologist Neil M. Judd of the National Museum. About 7000 individuals lived in Chaco Canyon in the 1000s and early 1100s.

(A Gauche) PALAIS DES ROCHERS, PARC NATIONAL, MESA VERDE, Colorado

(左) メサ・ヴァデ 国立公園内 岩壁宮殿

(Links) FELSENPALAST, MESA VERDE NATIONAL PARK, Colorado

(Left) CLIFF PALACE, MESA VERDE NATIONAL PARK, Colorado
Under the protective cover of overhanging rock, the remains of near perfect square and round towers, kivas and living rooms rise in the light of late afternoon sunlight.

(A Droite) BETATAKIN, MONUMENT NATIONAL NAVAJO

(右) ナヴァホ 国有記念物 内 ベタタキン

(Rechts) BETATAKIN, NAVAJO NATIONAL MONUMENT

(Right) BETATAKIN, NAVAJO NATIONAL MONUMENT
These ruins in a mammoth cave are one of the three largest cliff dwellings known. Its inhabitants of some 800 years ago utilized solar heating since the cliff overhang provided shade in the summer and winter's low sun warmed the red sandstone. It was not discovered until 1909 and contained about 200 rooms.

(Page 14) WALPI, UN VILLAGE HOPI, PREMIÈRE MESA

(十四頁) ワルピ, ホピ村　第一メサ

(Seite 14) WALPI, EINER DER HOPI SIEDLUNGEN, ERSTE MESA

(Page 14) WALPI, HOPI VILLAGES, FIRST MESA
(Photographed January 3, 1946 with permission from Chief Ned)
This village in the sky remains almost the way it was hundreds of years ago. There are no power or telephone poles or television antennas. Photography has long been prohibited.

(Page 15) SOMMETS DES MONTAGNES SAN FRANCISCO

(十五頁) サン・フランシスコ 山脈

(Seite 15) DIE SAN FRANCISCO BERGE

(Page 15) THE SAN FRANCISCO PEAKS
Golden light at sunset seems to warm the frosted top of this 12,670 foot high volcano. North of Flagstaff, Arizona's highest mountain peaks are sacred to both the Hopi and Navajo.

(*A Gauche*) WUPATKI, MONUMENT NATIONAL

(十六頁) ウパットキ
国有記念物

WUPATKI NATIONAL MONUMENT

(*Left*) WUPATKI NATIONAL MONUMENT
Occupied about 700 years ago, this ruin once contained nearly 100 rooms. The Ancient Ones used whatever building material was at hand.

(*Page 17*) LA VALLÉE MONUMENT, PARC DE LA TRIBU NAVAJO
(8 photographies)

(十七頁) モニュメント・ヴァレー
ナヴァホ部族公園

(*Page 17*) MONUMENT VALLEY NAVAJO TRIBAL PARK
(8 photographs)

PARK DES NAVAJO STAMMES IN MONUMENT VALLEY
(8 Bilder)

(*A Droite*) LES MITAINES

指無し手袋（写真八枚）

DIE FÄUSTLINGE

(*Right*) THE MITTENS
A winter snowfall comes to Navajoland, and to be there when the sun appears after the storm passes is an experience as great as seeing this wonderland for the first time.

(A Gauche) MITAINE DE GAUCHE

（左）指無し手袋 左手

(Links) DER LINKE FÄUSTLING

(Left) THE LEFT MITTEN
These sandstone remnants are all that
remain of a 1200 foot high plateau made
from windblown sand dunes solidified
ages ago.

(A Droite) POTEAU TOTÉMIQUE

（右）トーテム・ポール

(Rechts) DER TOTEMPFAHL
　　　(Yei-bi-chei Gruppe)

(Right) THE TOTEM POLE
　　　(Yei-bi-chei group)
Photogenic from many directions, this
formation is probably the most unusual
to be found anywhere in the Colorado
River basin.

(Pages 20–21) LA FENÊTRE DU NORD

（二十，二十一頁）北窓

(Seite 20–21) DAS NORDFENSTER

(Page 20–21) THE NORTH WINDOW
This framed viewpoint is one of the most
popular, giving a wide scope of the
valley. Sandstone monoliths dominate
the view. Summer clouds and shadows
give depth to this vast park, and in
winter an occasional snowfall creates a
new mood.

(A Gauche) LE HOGAN DE
SUZIE YAZZIE

（左）スージー・ヤージーさんの
ホガン

(Links) HOGAN DER SUSIE YAZZIE

(Left) SUSIE YAZZIE'S HOGAN
A twelve inch snowfall is rare in a
land that receives only five inches of
moisture a year. The log and mud home
offers excellent insulation and was the
traditional architecture until recently.

(A Droite) LES TROIS BONNES SOEURS

（右）三人姉妹

(Rechts) DIE DREI NONNEN

(Right) THE THREE SISTERS
These sandstone formations have been
named for visual interpretation of the
viewer and are among 72 so classified.

(A Gauche) L'OREILLE DU VENT

(左) 風の耳

(Links) DAS OHR DES WINDES

(Left) EAR OF THE WIND
A beautiful description of a colorful part of the heart of Monument Valley. Nearby is Moccasin Arch and the Sun's Eye.

(A Droite) LES SOURCES DE SABLE

(右) 砂州の泉

(Rechts) DIE SANDQUELLEN

(Right) SAND SPRINGS
Here is the valley's only permanent water supply where sheep and cattle can come for water. The wind replaces the sand's wavelets nearly every day.

(Page 26) LE ROCHER À LA FENÊTRE

（二十六頁） ウインドー・ロック

(Seite 26) DAS FENSTERSTEIN

(Left) WINDOW ROCK
This natural arch gave the Navajo's the name for their tribal headquarters. Window Rock is the most heavily populated area on the sprawling reservation.

(Page 27) GRAND FALLS,
   Little Colorado River
   (Grandes Chutes)

（二十七頁） グランド・フォール
（大瀑布）, 小 コロラド河

(Seite 27) GRAND FALLS,
   Little Colorado River

(Right) GRAND FALLS,
   Little Colorado River
Heavy summer rains and winter's melted snow increase the flow of this magnificent six hundred foot wide chocolate-colored falls. It was created by a lava flow that dammed the stream. The returning waters cascade back into the original stream bed creating falls higher than Niagara.

LE LAC POWELL, GLEN CANYON, RÉGION, NATIONALE DE RECRÉATION

グレン・キャニオン国立
レクリエーション地内 パウエル沽
（写眞二枚）

LAKE POWELL, GLEN CANYON NATIONALES ERHOLUNGSGEBIET

LAKE POWELL, GLEN CANYON NATIONAL RECREATION AREA

Many people feel this is the world's most unique lake. It has 1800 miles of sandstone shoreline. Its canyons, buttes, and tapestried walls change with every lighting condition, inviting exploration.

LE PONT L'ARC-EN-CIEL

虹 橋

DIE REGENBOGENBRÜCKE

RAINBOW BRIDGE

Fifty miles from Glen Canyon Dam, this, the world's largest natural span is truly a natural wonder. Nearby is domed Navajo Mountain, sacred to the Indians. A recent survey has set the bridge's height at 290 feet and its width at 275 feet, slightly less than the 1909 figures.

(Pages 30–31) TEMPÊTE DE NEIGE, GRAND CANYON, PARC NATIONAL

（三十,三十一頁） グランド・キャニオン
国立公圜の 吹雪（写眞六枚）

(Seite 30–31) SCHNEESTURM, GRAND CANYON NATIONAL PARK

(Page 30–31) SNOW STORM, GRAND CANYON NATIONAL PARK

A winter storm crosses the Canyon in its fury, approaching Bright Angel Creek. The views from the South Rim are everchanging and occasionally after a heavy snowfall, the Canyon is white nearly to the bottom. The endless variety of the Canyon moods, winter storms, summer lightning, early morning mist, fog and late afternoon shadows give the visitor endless scenes of an overwhelming spectacle.

(A Gauche) LE FLEUVE COLORADO

（左）コロラド河

(Links) DER COLORADO

(Left) THE COLORADO RIVER
A river run or a hike into the depths of the Grand Canyon gives the true feeling of its depth. The mule ride to Phantom Ranch or just to the inner gorge is safe and will make your visit truly memorable.

(A Droite) DES OMBRES SUR LE GRAND CANYON

（右）グランド・キャニオン 峡谷の影

(Rechts) SCHATTEN IM GRAND CANYON

(Right) GRAND CANYON SHADOWS
Endless changes in the Canyon's mood are caused by varying light, color, and texture. Most photographers cringe when they observe visitors photographing it at midday, for the later afternoon light lengthens the shadows and reveals the immensity of the 13 mile-wide canyon.

(*A Gauche*) LE COUCHER DU SOLEIL SUR LE POINT HOPI

（左）ホピ地点に於ける夕焼け空

(*Links*) SONNENUNTERGANG AM HOPI
          AUSSICHTSPUNKT

(*Left*) SUNSET, HOPI POINT
Sunrise and sunset at the Grand Canyon may be described as
views into foreverness.

(*A Droite*) LA CASCADE DES GÉNIES, LE FLEUVE
          COLORADO

（右）妖精の瀧，コロラド河

(*Rechts*) WASSERFALL DER ELFEN AM COLORADO

(*Right*) ELF FALLS, COLORADO RIVER
Elves Chasm on Royal Arch Creek is a fairyland of beauty just
before it enters the river. It is always in soft shadowed light but
receives reflected light from canyon walls.

(A Gauche) RÉGION RÉSERVÉE AUX INDIENS
HAVASUPAI, GRAND CANYON (4 photographies)
NAVAJO CASCADE

(左) グランド・キャニオン内 ハヴァスパイ・インデアン
指定保留地, ナヴァホ瀑布

(Links) HAVASUPAI INDIANER RESERVAT,
GRAND CANYON (4 Bilder)

NAVAJO WASSERFALL

(Left) HAVASUPAI INDIAN RESERVATION, GRAND CANYON
(four photographs)

NAVAJO FALLS
Travertine build-up, mosses, and vines contrast with the barren
walls of Havasu Creek. This is the first of the three largest falls
below Havasu Indian Village.

(A Droite) HAVASU CASCADE

(右) ハヴァス 瀑布

(Rechts) HAVASU WASSERFALL

(Right) HAVASU FALLS
Many who have spent several days in this Land of Sky-blue Waters
feel this pool is part of a true paradise. Violent flash floods
sometimes change the shape of the falls.

(A Gauche) MOONEY CASCADE

（左）ムーニー瀑布

(Links) MOONEY WASSERFALL

(Left) MOONEY FALLS
The highest of the three major falls, it spills over into emerald pools of travertine. Cottonwoods are encrusted with deposited residue as the windblown mist dries on their surfaces.

(A Droite) HAVASU CASCADE

（右）ハヴァス瀑布

(Rechts) HAVASU WASSERFALL

(Right) HAVASU FALLS
Travertine dams hold the cascading turquoise water in everchanging ponds.

(*A Guache*) PETRIFIED FOREST (LA
FORÊT PÉTRIFIÉE)

（四十頁）石化森林

国立公園（写眞四枚）

(*Links*) PETRIFIED FOREST
(VERSTEINERTE WALD)
NATIONAL PARK

(*Left*) PETRIFIED FOREST
NATIONAL PARK
Sections of two pedestal rock logs are
exposed that were covered with clay 180
million years ago. Once trees grew here
in giant sizes, an everglades that would
seem preposterous were it not for the
evidence lying on the ground.

(*A Droite*) MESA BLEUE

（四十一頁）ブルー・メサ

(*Rechts*) BLAUE MESA

(*Right*) BLUE MESA
While making this photograph, a small
segment of clay sloughed from the support. The Blue Mesa is a painted desert
of strange, eroded clay and shale.

(A Gauche) TERRAIN DES LONGS
TRONCS D'ARBRE

(左) 長い丸太周辺

(Links) GEBIET DER LANGEN STÄMME

(Left) LONG LOGS AREA
These colorful segments from a prehistoric forest are preserved in silica, colored by magnesium and oxides of iron.

(A Droite) LE PONT CASSÉ

(右) 毀れた橋

(Rechts) GEBROCHENE BRÜCKE

(Right) BROKEN BRIDGE
Ages of erosion have slowly revealed segments of these colorful logs; several span small gullies.

(A Gauche) LES FORTIFICATIONS
DES COCHISE

（左）コケーズ要塞

(Links) FELSENFESTUNG DES COCHISE

(Left) COCHISE STRONGHOLD
Rugged canyons and secluded valleys
provided refuge for the Apaches from
their enemies. In this area there are
many unusual granite formations,
including balanced rocks and forms that
could be named such as potatoes,
dragons, toadstools, etc.

(A Droite) LE BÉTAIL EN ROUTE

（右）アパッケー の 牛追リ

APACHE VIEHTRIEB

(Right) APACHE CATTLE DRIVE
The Apaches have superior herds of
cattle and when they are brought down
from the high country they are driven
across Whiteriver near Fort Apache.

44

(*A Gauche*) CHAMPIGNON ROCHERS, MONUMENT
    NATIONAL CHIRICAHUA

（左）チリカワ国有記念物内　キノコ

PILZFELSEN, CHIRICAHUA NATIONAL MONUMENT

(*Left*) MUSHROOMS ROCKS, CHIRICAHUA NATIONAL
    MONUMENT
Huge balanced rocks and eroded volcanic formations form the
uniqueness of this wonderland of rocks.

(*A Droite*) LE LAC DE RIGGS, MONTAGNES GRAHAM,
    FORÊT NATIONALE, COLORADO

（右）コロラド国有森林内
リッグズ湖とグレアム山

(*Rechts*) RIGGS LAKE, GRAHAM MOUNTAIN,
    CORONADO NATIONAL FOREST

(*Right*) RIGGS LAKE, GRAHAM MOUNTAIN, CORONADO
    NATIONAL FOREST
This man-made lake lies high on one of the desert islands in the
sky that comprise a part of the forest.

(A Gauche) LE CHÂTEAU DE MONTEZUMA, MONUMENT NATIONAL

（左）モンテズマ城
国有記念物

(Links) MONTEZUMAS SCHLOß NATIONAL MONUMENT

(Left) MONTEZUMA CASTLE NATIONAL MONUMENT
There is no connection with the former emperor of Mexico. A large limestone cave was the beginning for this twenty room, five story cliff dwelling that was occupied between the 8th and 14th centuries by a people called the Sinagua.

(A Droite) TUMACACORI, MONUMENT NATIONAL

（右）ツマカコリ国有記念物

(Rechts) TUMACACORI NATIONAL MONUMENT

(Right) TUMACACORI NATIONAL MONUMENT
Colonial Spanish settlement of the Tubac region in 1691 was responsible for this mission called San Jose de Tumacacori.

(A Gauche) LE ROCHER DE LA CATHÉDRALE

（五十頁） オーク・クリーク の

大寺院岩

(Links) DIE CATHEDRALE

(Left) CATHEDRAL ROCK

This scene at Redrock Crossing on Oak Creek would be hard to duplicate anywhere. The sandstone spires are impressive and doubly enhanced by the clear water crossing layers of sandstone.

(A Droite) LE ROCHER GLISSANT, OAK CREEK

（五十一頁） オーク・クリーク の 滑り岩

(Rechts) DIE RUTSCHBAHN, OAK CREEK

(Right) SLIDE ROCK, OAK CREEK

A popular summertime recreation area where waters flow smoothly over strata of sandstone making a natural slide. In winter it is a fairyland of frigid beauty.

(A Gaucho) LES RUINES
DE CASA GRANDE,
MONUMENT NATIONAL

（左）カサ・グランデ廃墟
国有記念物

(Links) CASA GRANDE RUINEN
NATIONAL MONUMENT

(Left) CASA GRANDE RUINS
NATIONAL MONUMENT
The Big House, built by the Saladoans about 1350 is a multi-storied house that would melt into the earth it came from if not sheltered. It had no natural protective cave as did most all other prehistoric Indian dwellings.

(A Droite) LA MISSION SAN XAVIER

（右）
聖 ザヴィエル・ミッション

(Rechts) SAN XAVIER MISSION

(Right) SAN XAVIER MISSION
The glaring white plastered surface of the adobe structure can be seen for great distances across the Papago fields that surround it. Still an active church, it was founded in 1692. Since restoration it has served the San Xavier Papago Indian people since 1797.

(A Gauche) LES MONTAGNES SANTA
CATALINA

（左）サンタ・カタリナ 山脈

(Links) DIE SANTA CATALINAS

(Left) SANTA CATALINA MOUNTAINS
At sunset the grey mountains turn purple
and gold. Many photographers feel this is
the most glorious time of the day. The
saguaro is filled with warmth of late evening
light.

(A Droite) SABINO CANYON

（右）サビノ・キャニオン

(Rechts) SABINO CANYON

(Right) SABINO CANYON
Sabino Creek drains a portion of the Santa
Catalina mountain range. It is an unusual
haven and in the fall, which comes usually
in December, the cottonwoods and syca-
mores help define the season.

(Pages 56–57) LA VALLÉE AVRA

（五十六，五十七頁）
アヴラ 盆地

(Seite 56–57) AVRA VALLEY

(Page 56-57) AVRA VALLEY
Summer rains usually come like a mon-
soon, flooding spots and leaving other
areas without rainfall. Tnese thunder
storms are a welcome sight for the Papago,
for they now graze large herds of fine cattle. It is also the time of most spectacular
sunsets.

(A Gauche) LES PAVOTS DE SONORA,
RÉGION RÉSERVÉE AUX PAPAGO

(左) パパゴ インデアン
指定保留地 内 ソノラ罌粟

(Links) SONORA MOHNBLUMEN,
PAPAGO INDIANER RESERVAT

(Left) SONORA POPPIES, PAPAGO
RESERVATION
Near Kitt Peak National Observatory, this vast
area abounds in a great variety of wild flowers
each spring if winter rains are sufficient.

(A Droite) CIERGE MEXICAIN, MONUMENT
NATIONAL

(右) オルガン・パイプ
国有記念物 (写真四枚)

(Hechts) ORGELPFEIFEN KAKTEEN
NATIONAL MONUMENT

(Right) ORGAN PIPE NATIONAL MONUMENT
The Ajo mountain drive offers the finest
opportunity to see the rugged beauty of this land
near the Mexican border.

(Page 60) LES MONTAGNES AJO

(六十頁) アホ 山脈

(Seite 60) DIE AJO BERGE

(Page 60) AJO MOUNTAINS
The drive toward the monument entrance is
exceptionally beautiful in late afternoon. The giant
saguaro gradually is joined with the organ pipe
cactus. This is the only organ pipe cactus forest in
the world.

(Page 61) PONT NATUREL

(六十一頁) 自然橋

(Seite 61) NATÜRLICHE BRÜCKE

(Page 61) NATURAL BRIDGE
Two small volcanic bridges accent one of the
highlights of the East Loop drive through the Ajo
mountains in the monument.

Gauche) CIERGES MEXICAINS

...上）

...ルガン・パイプ型 サボテン

...ks) ORGELPFEIFEN KAKTEEN

...ft) ORGAN PIPE CACTUS

...s area has over 30 varieties of cactus and 225
...ecies of birds. Some of these strange plants
...w 25 feet tall.

...Droite) ORAGE SUR TUCSON

...右）ツーソン市上 の 稲妻

...echts) GEWITTER ÜBER TUCSON

...ight) LIGHTNING OVER TUCSON

...nds and lightning precede a typical desert
...understorm. Though dangerous, the lightning
...play is often spectacular. (Photo by Alan
...anley.)

...age 64) LA MISSION SAN XAVIER DEL BAC
(La Colombe Blanche du désert)

...六十四頁）

...里 ザヴィエル ・ ミッション

...eite 64) SAN XAVIER MISSION DEL BAC (Die weiße
Taube der Wüste)

...age 64) SAN XAVIER MISSION DEL BAC
...e White Dove of the Desert.

Ray Manley's INDIAN LANDS
Text by Clara Lee Tanner

Indian Lands are lands of beauty, lands of great antiquity, lands of ever-changing character. At sunrise or sunset, in the full blast of a summer's day or covered with snow, whether carved and colorful or flat and colorless, they are lands of charm. All of Arizona and parts of adjoining states, at one time or another, in the past or today, have comprised lands occupied by Indians.

This incomparable country can be divided into three large sections; the northern Plateau, a central Mountain section, and the southern Desert area. In turn, the three differing environments nurtured three major native ancient cultures; Anasazi, Mogollon, and Hohokam, respectively. Each culture adapted to the vagaries of its area, blending homes into cliff sides or desert sands, cultivating foodstuffs to supplement hunting wild game, always becoming a part of the beloved land in which they lived. So much a part of this land did they become that some have survived to this day, Anasazis as puebloans, and some Hohokams as represented by the Pimas and Papagos. Although the Mogollons dispersed, the blood of some still flows in veins of certain puebloan tribes of the Rio Grande Valley. Further, a few "newcomers," the Apaches and Navajos, became equally adapted to these lands.

Plateau lands are dominantly of elevations between 5000' to 7000' with some quite high points including, among others, the 13,000' San Francisco Peaks and 10,000' Navajo Mountain. Certainly the beautiful San Francisco Peaks are worthy to be the homeland of Hopi spirits, the kachinas. Often parts of the Plateau, which was formed by deposits of inland seas, eons ago, have been heavily weathered, forming fantastic and beautiful buttes and pinnacles, red-walled mesas, deep, sheer-walled, and vari-colored canyons.

In northeastern Arizona is Canyon de Chelly, with its red walls and irregularly cut-out caves, large and small, and that spectacular pinnacle, Spider Rock. Canyon del Muerto is close by, with the two canyons joining, both housing ancient populations in their many protective caves. Other canyons simulate these two in their sheer red walls and inviting caves, including those of Navajo National Monument, with more villages nestled in the caves. To the east, in northwestern New Mexico, is the beginning of the San Juan Valley, parts of which present equally colorful canyon walls.

Then to the west but still in northeastern Arizona is Monument Valley, always beautiful in its dominantly red formations, but spectacular at sunset or when blanketed with snow. It took wind and weather many millenia to carve buttes such as the Mittens, or the slender Totem Pole, or even to hollow out the Ear of the Wind, a natural bridge. On either side of this wide valley are great cliffs, never so close as to press on the viewer, and always responding, like the other formations, to light and shadow, to full sun and snow.

Some of the red formations continue on to the west, often in totally different aspects. To be sure, there is many another canyon, sometimes red-walled, sometimes creating narrow chasms of delicately hued and of varied formations. Such is the country leading to the almost 300' high Rainbow Bridge in southern Utah, a great natural "beautiful arch," a translation of the Navajo word "Nonnezoshi Boko." Today the extensive waters of man-made Lake Powell lap onto the rocks at the base of Rainbow Bridge, or, in other directions, cover much of the walls and even sweep up into caves once occupied by prehistoric men. South and into east Central Arizona the red formations are often soft appearing as wind and weather have worn down the sharper cliffs to rounded "haystacks" as they are called in the Window Rock area. Here too, is another natural window which inspired the name of this Navajo center.

Certainly one of the wonders of the world is the result of even greater and longer wearing by wind and weather, the Grand Canyon of Arizona. The geological history of the earth is dramatically related in the side walls of this Canyon, stratum beneath stratum from the present down to the oldest archaeozoic rocks. As one travels down Bright Angel Trail he is well aware of these stories in stone. Grand Canyon proper and sometimes the branches are wonderfully colorful, with distance often fading brighter hues into pale but rich blues, reds, purples, and other tones. A great storm over the Canyon adds to its vigor, its mystery, its endless nature, while snow brings into focus its quiet eternity.

From the Canyon top, the river (a mile below) seems but a thread. Beautiful waterfalls occur along the course of the great river. Some are so gossamer thin that they are veil-like, some are rushing torrents. Some are single, narrow, graceful mists of water. Where rock formations are in step-like patterns, the water tumbles down in one fall after the other, with occasional whirlpools of water forming as though to catch its breath.

There are endless branches leading into the Grand Canyon, some narrow and short, some lengthy, winding, and of several parts. Such is Havasu Canyon. In one part of this beautiful area are the Havasu Falls; in another are the Mooney Falls. Elf Falls is a most appropriate name for falls in a third canyon. Here the water seems to lilt gracefully from one boulder to the next, like a small, imaginary creature jumping about. Waters of these branch canyons support a great deal of greenery, from grasses and flowers to shrubs and trees. Many such a spot is a haven of refuge and a delight to the soul.

Volcanic activity was not unknown in these Indian lands and there are many surviving testimonials to this side of nature. There are extensive lava beds some miles east of Gallup, New Mexico. There are volcanic necks, one called Agathlas Needle at the southern entrance to Monument Valley, another in northeastern New Mexico which, because of its shape, is called Shiprock. Then there is Sunset Crater near Flagstaff, Arizona, which erupted about 1066, spewing out ash which enriched the lands for agricultural purposes.

Mixed in with all the spectacular cliffs, buttes, canyons, and other formations are quantities of sand. Sands occur at the base of many of the monuments, forming hills and waves of dunes. Here and there they fill the washes. In some places, particularly in canyons, there are dangerous quick sands which man and beast have learned to conquer.

Throughout the Plateau area there were temperature and rainfall variations, but withal, the higher altitude invited lower temperatures and more rainfall and snow. These combined conditions invited the growth of large trees, such as aspen which appear in abundance in the Flagstaff area and spottily elsewhere in the Plateau. Sporadic in distribution also are pine, piñon, and other high elevation trees, many of them supplying the Indians with building materials and firewood. A great variety of lesser plant growth offered the natives materials such as yucca and rabbit brush for basketry, or woods and stems for tools, weapons, implements, or they were sources of foods and medicines.

Altitude and available plant growth of the Plateau also affected the animal life which in turn affected the Indians. There was more large game here than in the Desert. To the extreme northeast were buffalo. Variously distributed otherwise were deer, antelope, bear, coyotes, rabbit, and many another creature. Some of these supplied the native with clothing, food, bone for tools, and, not the least in importance, characters in their legendary history and mythology. Most of these creatures have survived to the present moment; some continue to play a larger or smaller part in Indian life to say nothing of contributing to white man's pleasures as well.

Plateau lands were widely occupied by prehistoric folk called by archaeologists "Anasazi" which means the "ancient ones." This was their homeland from shortly after the opening of the Christian Era. Starting by occupying natural caves without benefit of much in the way of artificial construction except storage bins, they went through several stages of building and of development of their culture. The first dwellers in caves cultivated corn and undoubtedly supplemented their diet with both native plants and animals. In time they added beans and squash—and did less hunting and gathering. As they became settled they built pit houses into the ground, in a sense, little more than elaborated storage bins. Agriculture brought a certain prosperity, and with prosperity, they moved their homes to ground level. In the beginning of this trend houses were of one story and limited in number, but in time and in some centers, populations increased to the degree that large villages were needed.

Now full-fledged "pueblos," stepped, multi-storied, and many-roomed, were built in one unit like an apartment house. Some were constructed in open areas such as the magnificent masonry-walled Wupatki. This and many other ruins are located in Wupatki National Monument north of Flagstaff. Many of the ancients built on more limited Mesa tops, such as Segazlin Mesa near Navajo Mountain which accommodated one row of rooms and a second pueblo cluster. Valleys large or small were sought out by others, perhaps because of more abundant and closer water resources, for many such locations had running streams. Chaco Canyon was a favored spot, probably offering both water and trees which are absent today. Pueblo Bonito was one of the great ruins of this area, with its village constructed in D-shape, the straight side but one story in height, the rounded portion rising to five stories, and with a completely enclosed plaza or courtyard. Within the court and also mixed in with the joined rooms were large and small, round, and semi-underground rooms called kivas. These were common in prehistoric pueblos and were used for secret and other religious rites. The architecture at Pueblo Bonito was some of the finest in the prehistoric Southwest.

Perhaps the most picturesque of prehistoric Plateau pueblos were those constructed in caves at lower or higher points along cliffs. Near Flagstaff is Walnut Canyon ruin, a single row of one story rooms, for the ledges on which they were located would accommodate no more. In Canyon de Chelly were many ruins in caves, including multi-storied White House and Antelope House in del Muerto. White House was constructed partially at the base of the cliff, then stories above led to a large section built within the cave. Mesa Verde, in southwestern Colorado, has many ruins in larger or smaller caves in sandstone walls, often multi-storied and with kivas amongst the rooms of the pueblos. Cliff Palace is a good example of this.

In the Segie Canyon, Navajo National Monument, are two important and large ruins, Betatakin and Kietsiel. Both are built in large scooped-out caves, with some of Betatakin's rooms dribbling out a little beyond, virtually hugging the cliff wall. There were many other villages located in canyons, including smaller ones in branches of the Grand Canyon.

Seemingly many of these pueblo folk made a good living for themselves in this colorful land. Undoubtedly there was more water in parts of the country than there is today, and perhaps more or differently distributed animals and plant life. Certainly there was enough for most of these stone age folk, for populations did not become too great. Literally they lived "off the land" for they supplied everything in their lives in the way of shelter, food, clothing, tools, and weapons, and even some luxury items such as jewelry.

Before the Spaniards arrived in the Southwest in 1540, puebloan populations had greatly decreased and had withdrawn from their widespread distribution to concentrate in three areas, many groups in the upper Rio Grande, the Zunis in western New Mexico, and Hopis in northeastern Arizona. Two smaller non-pueblo tribes, the Havasupai and Walapai, were located at this time to the west of the Grand Canyon. Also, some newcomers had arrived, preceding the Spaniards by perhaps several centuries. These were the Apaches and Navajos. All of these tribes have remained important to this day, and all but the Apaches have favored the Plateau as their homeland.

Hopi Indians represent a direct line from prehistoric Anasazi folk who continued to live on Plateau lands into historic years. There is such a gradual merging of the ancients into what are later called Hopis that there is really no end for one, no beginning of the other. Such ancient sites as Sikyatki were occupied by folk who had become thoroughly adjusted to the rigors of the mesas and flat lands of these barren parts of the Plateau. Hopis inherited this invaluable knowledge.

Hopi Indians gradually adapted their villages to the southern finger-like tips of Black Mesa. Here they lived the year around, the men daily running down to cultivate the clan lands below the mesas. In the fall, produce was carried up the steep trails to be stored in inner chambers of the family home. Each family, through the mother, had one or more rooms in one of the several structures which formed the pueblo.

These villages were constructed of the stones of the mesa itself, thus, frequently they seemed to melt into the native formations. In some instances the only break between cliff and structural walls was an occasional ladder sticking out of a kiva (ceremonial chamber) or leaning against a house. To these homes, Spanish contact added wooden doors, glazed windows, and chimneys for the interior corner fireplace. In many Hopi homes it was not until much later that household furnishing became common.

In the craft arts the Hopis depended greatly on their environment for materials. For basketry, they used yucca, rabbit brush, and sumac primarily. Clay was distributed in abundance close at hand also. When kachina carving became important, probably in the last half of the nineteenth century, the Hopis began to use cottonwood root which had washed down the arroyos from Black Mesa. Today the same material is used. From prehistoric times, the ancestors of the Hopis had cultivated cotton; they continued to do so into the 1930s as this material was a requisite for ceremonial garments woven by the men. Commercial cotton then replaced the native variety.

Hopi Indians are familiar with and have names for more than one hundred native plants, a testimonial to the centuries they have occupied this area. In addition to those used for crafts, others were important in the production of tools, weapons, implements, and ceremonial objects. Too, some added to the variety of the diet of these Indians, and many were used for medicinal and ritual purposes.

So beloved is this land to the Hopi Indians that, to the last man, they wish to return to their native village before death overtakes them.

In a manner comparable to that of the Hopi, but with more direct contact with Spaniards, the pueblos of Zuñis and the Rio Grande developed into the historic period. Their homes acquired doors, windows, interior fireplaces, and household furnishings sooner than did the Hopis. And, although they maintained their own native religion, much of it secretly practiced, the Rio Grande pueblos in particular were required to worship in Catholic chapels.

The acquisition of Indian country by Anglo-Americans in time resulted in many changes in the Rio Grande: formal education, commercial cloth which wiped out weaving, pots and pans which practically cut out basketry and cut down on ceramic production (later revived for commercial purposes), new forms of tribal government, and farming with big machinery. Changes have occurred in some of their villages, such as abandoning the style of pueblo construction, as noted at Jémez. Some inroads have been made on their religion too, for example, white man's medicine has affected some curing rites, or big farm machinery, better water control, and fertilization of fields have negated some native dances for rain and crop maturation.

One village which has retained its original form and much of its native life to a greater degree is Taos. This pueblo is the northernmost of all in the Rio Grande. It preserves the pueblo style of architecture, with its two age-old, large units of five story rooms on each side of the river which runs through the village. Taos is particularly beautiful with its large pueblo units silhouetted against a high mountain range. Zuñi, on the other hand, has a highway running through the center of the village. Slight wonder that the old pueblo style has been partially replaced by individual homes. Not surprising, too, are abundant automobiles, bicycles, and motorcycles. So popular has been turquoise (or other stones) and silver jewelry of this tribe that quite a few Zuñis have made big money selling it. Yet some aspects of native life are retained: one of the most important is the annual presentation of Shalako which consumes months of time of the ceremonialists and adds much to the unity of the village.

Havasupais have not always lived the year around in lovely Havasu Canyon. As far back as they have been known historically in this area, they divided their time between the canyon and the mesa tops above. During the winter they roamed the higher lands, hunting and gathering to supplement a lean larder. In the spring they returned to the canyon bottom to plant their fields. However, as they learned better methods of farming, and as the mesa lands were not theirs alone to roam, they began to stay for longer periods in the canyon, in time becoming permanent residents. Now they say they will remain in Havasu Canyon until the two great rocks which mark the trail fall and are demolished.

Through the years the Havasupai Indians also bettered their way of life by learning to herd cattle. There was some feed in the Canyon, and they could cultivate a bit more. At one time they built simple grass and earth huts but later were able to construct more modern houses. The only entrance to this Indian settlement is the trail, by foot or horseback. However, helicopters have dropped a few additional items to the Havasupai, such as parts of an organ to be put in their church. It would seem that these Indians might be too isolated, lonely, out of contact with the world. However, the eternal beauty of red canyon walls and greenery, the comfort of protection of the two great rocks, a constant water supply, food for themselves and their animals—these are blessings enough! In addition they have many tourist visitors.

Havasupais have produced crafts along the way, both for themselves and for sale. A great open-mouthed, conical burden basket served them well as the women could sweep the seeds off the tops of local grasses into the containers. Some of these baskets were sold. In more recent years tourists who cherished a moment of the beauty of Havasu Canyon also purchased coiled baskets woven by the women of this tribe.

Close relatives of the Havasupai are the (Walapai) Hualapai Indians. They too have lived on the high lands and were in contact with their language brothers, the Havasupai. In fact, there has been much intermarriage between the two groups. Today the Hualapais still prefer the higher lands for grazing their cattle and for limited agriculture. Walapais also do some basketry, practically all of it sold to white men.

Despite the relatively recent arrival of the Navajos in the Southwest, their attitudes towards these lands are such that one can believe they have lived here forever. Legend says that they were created and destined to live here. Their great heroes, the Twin War Gods, killed giants which inhabited these lands; proof of this is cited in the volcanic neck, Shiprock, which is really the congealed blood of those giants.

The Navajos' cultural hero, Nayenezgani, went down a great river—probably the Colorado—and visited the yei, or gods. There he learned of the four sacred crops of the Southwest, corn, beans, squash, and tobacco. Further, he learned all about sandpaintings. In a great room there were clouds rolled up on shelves. For the young hero, they were unfurled on the floor, and on each was a beautiful design of a sandpainting. The hero was instructed to remember the pattern and the lore which went with each, to take all back to his people. Thus the paintings were to be carried in the minds of men only, never to be permanent.

Only a land of great beauty could incite such magnificent tales like the above, plus many more.

Navajos settled in New Mexico first, some in the San Juan valley where they left records on red sandstone walls of the very yei which later appear in their sandpaintings. In other parts of New Mexico are found remains of their hogan rings, evidences of their early occupation sites. Within some such sites are also found remains of small pueblos, evidence of the living together of Navajos and pueblo Indians. A more practical approach to explain the acquisition of knowledge pertaining to agricultural produce and ceremonies by the Navajos would be that they acquired them from the pueblo Indians. Nonetheless, the land aided and abetted the coloring of this knowledge with imagination and beauty.

After Spanish contact, the Navajo acquired horses and sheep. Herding and grazing the latter, plus riding the horses constantly, carried these Indians farther afield—eventually they were in Canyons de Chelly and del Muerto, then went on west into Monument Valley, and eventually onto Black Mesa. Few parts of northern Arizona were left untouched by Navajo occupation. Come snow, come wind, come any kind of weather—the Navajo loves this land and remains here. Whether occupied by one alone or by a large family, there are still individual hogans or two or three in a group In Monument Valley, in Canyon de Chelly, in all the spots favored by Navajos.

Abundant piñon and other growth supplied building material necessary for ever increasing numbers of hogans. Increased sheep encouraged weaving, and the ever beautiful environment piqued the imagination in the direction of developing design. For many decades this industry supplied clothing for the Navajos; Anglo contact brought ready-woven materials for clothing which displaced the need for hand-woven garments. However, this same contact gave incentive to further production of a heavier hand-loomed product which became the rug, thus the rug was commercialized. This, however, was no detriment to imaginative design.

At the time of World War II, surprising resources were discovered on the Navajo Reservation, including oil, gas, uranium, and vanadium. Monies from these sources have been intelligently used by the tribal council for the betterment of the entire group. Among other things they have aided in the construction of roads, schools, tribal industries, a museum, and craft guilds, all a part of the updating of the lives of these people.

The Mountain area lies between the Plateau to the north and the Desert to the south and southwest. As far as prehistoric occupation of the three areas was concerned, there was considerable overlapping of cultures, and even a little in historic times. The term "Mountain" tells much about this country, for it is characteristically rugged, with smaller flat areas than are found in either the Desert or the Plateau. Consequently, elevation, temperatures, snow, rainfall vary more, these in turn inviting variety in plant and animal life. Everything from cactus to aspen can be found in Mountain lands, plus all animal types from elk, bear, deer, to turkeys and rattlesnakes.

Dropping down from Flagstaff into Sedona country shows changes from pine and aspen to oak and cottonwood. The last of colorful red formations are in Sedona; here are Slide Rock north of town and beautiful Cathedral Rock to the south. To the east is Verde Valley, with Montezuma's Well one of the unusual natural spots here. Also on eastward and south is the Petrified Forest, with its great and small pieces of this wood, among others Balanced Log, the Blue Forest, and a bridge formed by a great prostrate petrified log. Indian ruins are found in this National Monument area.

The southern border of the Mountain area is marked by the deep and colorful Salt River Canyon. Farther east and into New Mexico is a branch of the Gila River, the San Francisco. Out of the Mountains proper and to the east of this is flat land, more desert-like in nature. Here a small river, the Mimbres, rises and quickly disappears.

Prehistoric populations of this Mountain country were numerous and widespread. Those belonging to the Mogollon proper are found more in the central and eastern sections, from the White Mountains to Mimbres country. As among the Anasazi, their pit houses were followed by small pueblo homes. Kivas were also used by these folk, although they differed in some ways from the typical Anasazi ceremonial room. Mogollon pottery may also have been influenced by Anasazi or Hohokam styles, or both, but in its last expressions in this area, the Mimbres, its wares were unique in their black and white (and sometimes yellow) bowls which presented many compositions. Otherwise, Mogollones were a comparable stone-age people, differing only as environment and contacts with others colored their culture.

When the Apaches entered the Southwest, they were probably quite nomadic; further association with the Plains Indians did not make them less so. For years the Apaches roamed far and wide over New Mexico and Arizona, and south into Mexico. They wandered throughout Chiricahua Mountain country, some "holed up" in Cochise Stronghold, some wandered west into the Tumacacori Mission and Papago territories. In fact, there were few spots in southern Arizona where Apaches did not roam.

After conflicts with Spaniards, Mexicans, and Anglo Americans, the Apaches were settled on two Reservations in east-central Arizona. Here they have remained ever since, with relatively small numbers of them leaving for "greener pastures."

Although their earlier years were based on hunting and raiding, with a little farming, the Apaches of the San Carlos reservation settled down to cattle raising, while those in the White Mountains did more farming and some herding. In time the latter group added tourist attractions to aid in their economy, building motels, lakes stocked with fish, lumber mills, and ski areas, among others. The San Carlos Apaches continued in cattle raising, producing some of the finest stock in the Southwest.

As part of their roving life, the Apaches were more basket weavers than potters. Where they settled down finally, they found ample materials to continue this craft. Both groups produced pitched water bottles, burden baskets, and coiled trays and jars. All but the last were used extensively until recent times; now but a few baskets are made and these largely for sale. Like other tribes, the Apaches have become involved in making a living not only by cattle raising and farming, but also as wage workers, lumbermen, by developing small industries. Even the women have become nurses and teachers, or work in industries such as the candle business developed by Apaches on the San Carlos Reservation.

Both Apache groups have Tribal Councils which are interested in developing their natural resources as well as in politics. These tribal leaders in many instances, have done a remarkable job in directing the development of their lands and people. Interest in higher education has also been an important factor in these matters.

Indian lands of the Desert are quite different indeed from those of the Plateau and Mountains. Average elevations run from 1,000' to 2,000' more or less above sea level. This, plus the fact that they are farther south, makes for higher temperatures, hot summers and warm, toasty winters. Characteristic of the Desert are short mountain ranges which run generally in a northwest-southeast direction. A few of these are around 8,000' to 9,000' and support limited growth more common to the north such as pine, maple, and even a bit of aspen. There are a few rivers in this Desert area, with the Gila and Salt most important. The Santa Cruz and the San Pedro seem to have been more important to the prehistoric natives than they now are. Parts of the Desert are devoid of any rivers whatsoever, such as the southwestern section of Arizona.

Desert growth, of course, is greatly different. Spiney plants dominate, with a great variety from cactus to mesquite. Most spectacular is the sahuaro, truly a giant in its full growth, with its great central trunk and a few or numerous "arms" as the cactus increases in age. Some live to be several hundreds of years old. Sahuaro trunk and arms are capped by beautiful white flowers, usually blooming in late May; these turn into a ruby red fruit. Even sticky chollas offer the natives a small bud which they dry and later soak and cook like beans.

Many desert plants supplied the natives with materials for their needs, such as yucca, bear grass, and desert willow for basketry. Although not as good as that in the Plateau, much clay was also found. Large trees were quite generally found in the mountains, thus materials for building were usually of poorer quality.

The Desert can be and often is dramatically spectacular. A thunder storm may be accompanied by lightning, silhouetting a sahuaro cactus in great beauty. Many of the Desert ranges are ever changing. The Catalinas near Tucson can be cardboard-flat, or the last ravine or formation will be magnified on a day when certain light and shadow play overhead, or a winter sunset can turn them into deep rose with stardust blue hiding in the canyons. So commanding is Baboquivari Peak to the southwest that it is worthy of the many legends that the Papagos have woven about it. Chiricahua National Monument in southeastern Arizona is a treasury of great boulders as several of them would testify, Balanced Rock, Mushroom Rock, and Big Rock. Near here is Cochise Stronghold, another rocky area which served to protect the Apache leader of this same name against his enemies.

Dry as the southwestern part of Arizona can be, it is often green and full of flowering plants. From the Tucson Mountains west through Avra Valley, past Kitt Peak and farther onto the Papago Reservation, this area can be a veritable wild garden. When rainfall has been abundant, grasses will abound, interrupted by masses of tiny yellow, orange, white, or purple flowerlettes growing close to the ground. Poppies appear in extensive patches, and along washes, Palo Verde trees will be turned into masses of gold. Many cacti will put forth their brilliant yellow, rose, purple, or burnt sienna blossoms. Farther west is the Organ Pipe National Monument with quantities of this unusual growth spreading for miles amidst mesquite and underbrush, all crowded when blessed with rainfall.

The prehistoric peoples of the Desert area were the Hohokams. Here these folk became established several centuries before the opening of the Christian era. Here they lived until about 1450. They built shallow pit houses, largely of oval form, with side walls of a few larger poles, such as mesquite, interspersed with small upright elements like ocotillo branches or sahuaro ribs, and all covered with earth (called wattle and daub). The River Hohokams, living in the Gila-Salt valleys, diverted the waters of these rivers into their great canals, thence onto their fields of corn, beans, and squash. The Desert Hohokam to the south where there were no rivers, eked out an existence by cultivating limited fields watered by rain or by diverted washes.

River Hohokams had a much richer culture, with highly developed pottery, elaborate shell work, stone carving, and with ceremonial centers involving platform mounds and ball courts. Desert Hohokams lagged behind in most culture traits. Both were a stone age people, having no knowledge of metals or metallurgy. Both were nature worshippers, interested in the control of water and weather, and, probably, disease. It is possible also that the River Hohokams evolved a chiefdom with one leader over several villages, perhaps necessary in order to enact control of water for the canals.

Sometime around 1400 a new people came into the River Hohokam area, from the north and east. They brought more sophisticated ideas of architecture, which resulted in the building of Casa Grande with its great thick-walled and multi-storied structure and compound-type enclosure. New types of pottery were introduced, plus other non-Hohokam traits. These two people, the Hohokams and the Saladoans as the newcomers are called, lived amicably together until the arrival of the Spaniards.

Spaniards built Tumacacori Mission where Papagos and Apaches sometimes met—not on the best of terms. Further north was constructed San Xavier Mission, with the help of the Papagos. The former is in ruins, the latter has served these Indians continuously since its building, with Papagos participating in all the services.

Pima Indians were perhaps more spread out in early historic times than they are today, although they were probably within irrigation distance of the rivers. As presumed descendants of the River Hohokam, it is likely that they inherited a rich agricultural economy, but later building of dams by white men above Pima lands curtailed this activity. Some amends have been made and some Pimas are still agriculturalists, today often using large machinery in the cultivation of fields. Some have become cattlemen. Others have turned to a variety of trades, to wage earning, or to other activities to make a living.

Homes of these Indian have changed greatly through the years. First, they continued to live for several centuries in the wattle-and-daub or adobe-walled huts which looked as though they virtually popped up out of the ground. Meeting of cultures has been evidenced in a shiny new car parked beside such a home, or a TV antenna atop its earthen roof! The one-roomed home became larger in time, with average two- and three-bedroom houses not uncommon today. Materials have changed from wattle-and-daub to bricks and concrete blocks, furnishings have moved from the native plaited mat to complete modern accommodations.

Like other Indian tribes, the Pimas have shifted from native government by chiefs to a strong Tribal Council. A fine building houses the activities of this group. Other community buildings on the Reservation include a hospital, Career Center, schools, and a child's day-care center. There is also a very fine Arts and Crafts center off Highway I-10, with a portion of the building given over to Pima history and culture.

Pimas lost much of their native culture sooner and faster than most of the Southwest Indians, perhaps in part because they were closer to larger white communities. Most of their craft expressions disappeared also, with some slight and occasional bit of pottery or basketry production. A recent revival of basketry has resulted in the production of some fine quality pieces.

Papago Indians have long lived on the most "desert" and riverless part of southern and southwestern Arizona. For centuries they have depended on rain-swollen arroyos for water to mature their crops. Testifying to this is the age-old June ceremony for the bringing of rain when sahuaro fruit wine is consumed in the company of Papago guests from other villages as a prayer to the spirits for water.

Cultivation of crops with limited moisture resulted in small harvests in the fall, so the Papagos retired to the mountains for the winter. Here they supplemented their lean larders by hunting deer, rabbits, and a few other creatures. Too, there was some water in the hills. Thus these Indians lived long after the arrival of the